Play the
SHAPE
GAME

BY THE CHILDREN'S LAUREATE
ANTHONY BROWNE

First published 2010 by Walker Books Ltd
87 Vauxhall Walk, London SE11 5HJ

2 4 6 8 10 9 7 5 3 1

Original shape and introduction by Anthony Browne.

This book has been produced in partnership with Waterstone's and Booktrust.

Shape contributions by
Hanne Bartholin, Sir Peter Blake, Quentin Blake, Alain de Botton, Jo Brand, Jim Carter,
Tracy Chevalier, Linford Christie, Richard Clifford, Lucy Cousins, Anne Fine,
Michael Foreman, Leigh Francis, Emily Gravett, John Hegley, Harry Hill, Anthony Horowitz,
Shirley Hughes, Sir Derek Jacobi, Phyllida Law, Ken Livingstone, Sam Lloyd, Ian McEwan,
Michael Morpurgo, Sir Andrew Motion, Patrick Ness, Tara Palmer-Tomkinson,
Jan Pieńkowski, Philip Pullman, Jane Ray, Catherine Rayner, Michael Rosen, Rob Ryan,
Axel Scheffler, Nick Sharratt, Andy Stanton, Imelda Staunton, Meera Syal, Alexis Taylor,
Emma Thompson, Hervé Tullet, Greg Wise, Marcia Williams, Dame Jacqueline Wilson
and Henry Winkler.

All profits from sales of this book are going to Rainbow Trust Children's Charity,
Registered Charity No.1070532

This book has been typeset in Gill Sans

Printed and bound in Great Britain by Butler Tanner & Dennis Ltd

British Library Cataloguing in Publication Data: a catalogue record for this
book is available from the British Library

ISBN: 978-1-4063-3131-8

www.walker.co.uk
www.rainbowtrust.org.uk
www.childrenslaureate.org.uk

Play the
SHAPE GAME

BY THE CHILDREN'S LAUREATE
ANTHONY BROWNE

WALKER BOOKS
AND SUBSIDIARIES
LONDON · BOSTON · SYDNEY · AUCKLAND

When my brother, Michael, and I were children, we invented two games.

The first involved throwing a ball to the top of the stairs, watching it bounce back down, and then catching it before it reached the ground. We played this game on many wet afternoons in West Yorkshire – a listless alternative to the more energetic outdoor pursuits for two bored but competitive little boys.

The other game we invented, the Shape Game, was far more interesting – so interesting, in fact, that I'm still playing it to this day. The rules of the Shape Game are very simple: the first player quickly draws any abstract shape at random, the second looks at it and then transforms it into something

(The shape everyone started with.)

recognizable. It could be anything – a face, a dinosaur or a fried egg. It could be a doodle or a work of fine art. When we were children, Michael and I thought this game was our invention, but having spoken to children all over the world, I have since discovered that children everywhere know it and play their own versions.

The wonderful thing about the Shape Game is that anyone with a little bit of imagination can join in. You don't have to be good at drawing to play and transform a shape. In this book, you'll find drawings by 45 well-known people, including artists, but also authors, actors, sports people, comedians and musicians. I gave them all exactly the same shape to play with, but as you'll see, their imaginations have led them in totally different directions. They have also drawn new shapes for you to transform, so you can join in and play the Shape Game along with us. Like the players in this book, you can use any materials, from a basic felt-tip pen to paints, crayons or collage. Turn the paper upside down or sideways, take as much or as little time as you want – simply let your imagination run wild and have fun!

All the proceeds from this book will be donated to Rainbow Trust Children's Charity, which provides vital support to families who have a child with a life threatening or terminal illness. I'm delighted about this because as Children's Laureate I want to help and connect with children everywhere, and encourage them to use their imaginations and be creative. Although it's just a simple game, I believe the Shape Game is the perfect way to do this. It encapsulates the act of creativity

– inspiration is everywhere.

I have played the Shape Game in every single book I have made, and now you have the chance to join in and play it, too. I hope you enjoy looking at the shapes in the book, and will love playing the Shape Game as much as I have!

Anthony Browne

Anthony Browne
Children's Laureate 2009–2011
www.childrenslaureate.org.uk

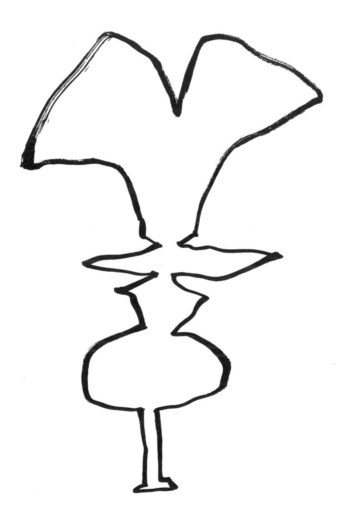

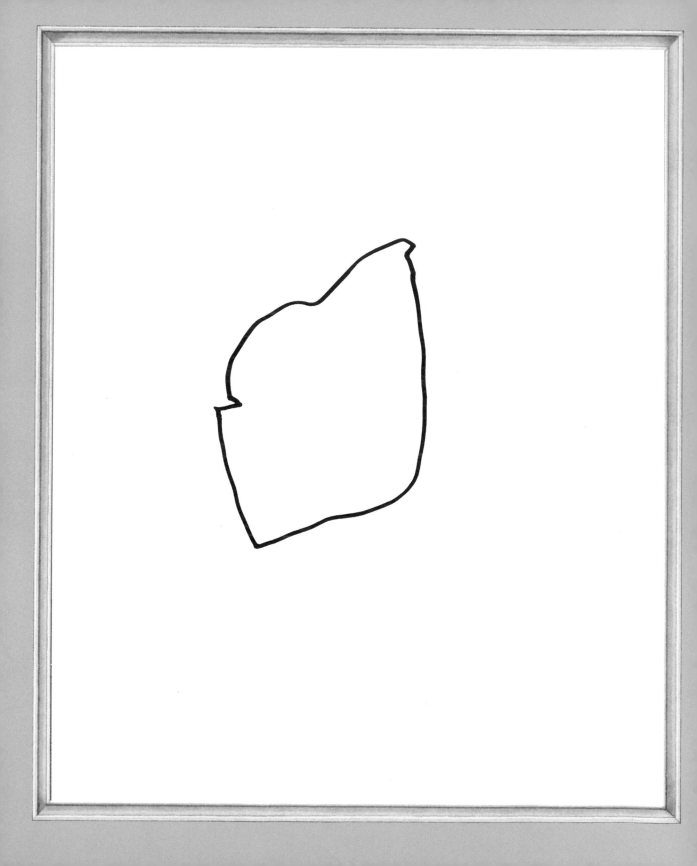

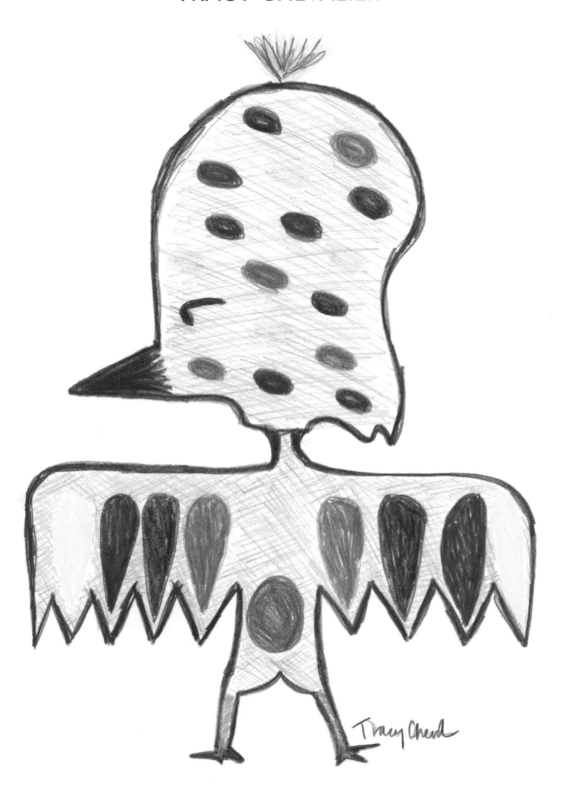

JO BRAND

Joke Generating Liquid

Heckle Neutraliser

Bun catcher In case people throw buns

GIANT TICKLING STICK

Video Screen To focus in on the miserable ones!

Protective Helmet For Stand Up Comedian

Jo Brand x

'Man in a Rainbow Hat'— For Rainbow Trust.   Peter Blake. 2010.

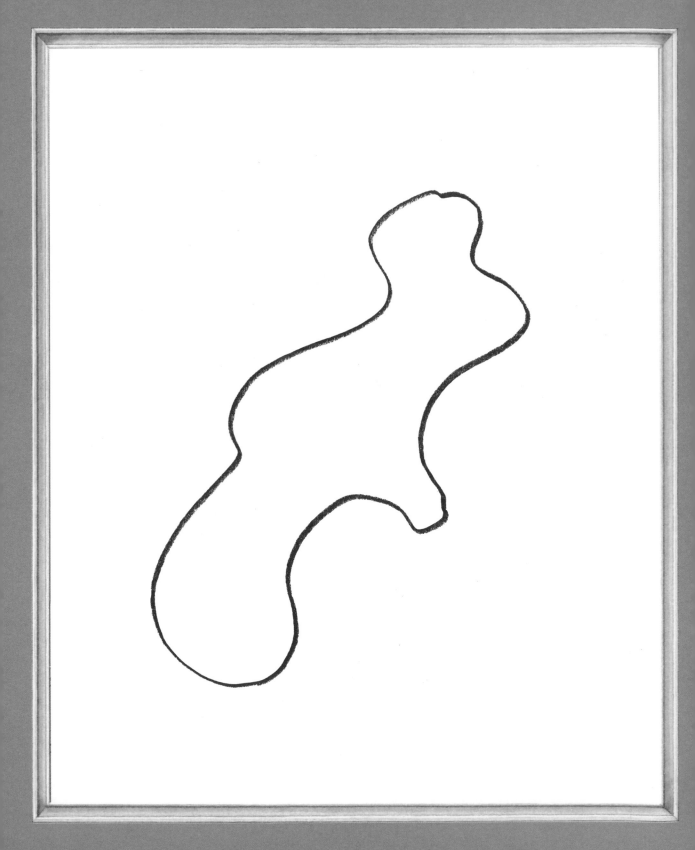

PHILIP PULLMAN

JAN PIEŃKOWSKI

ANTHONY HOROWITZ

A piano teacher wearing her new hat.

LINFORD CHRISTIE

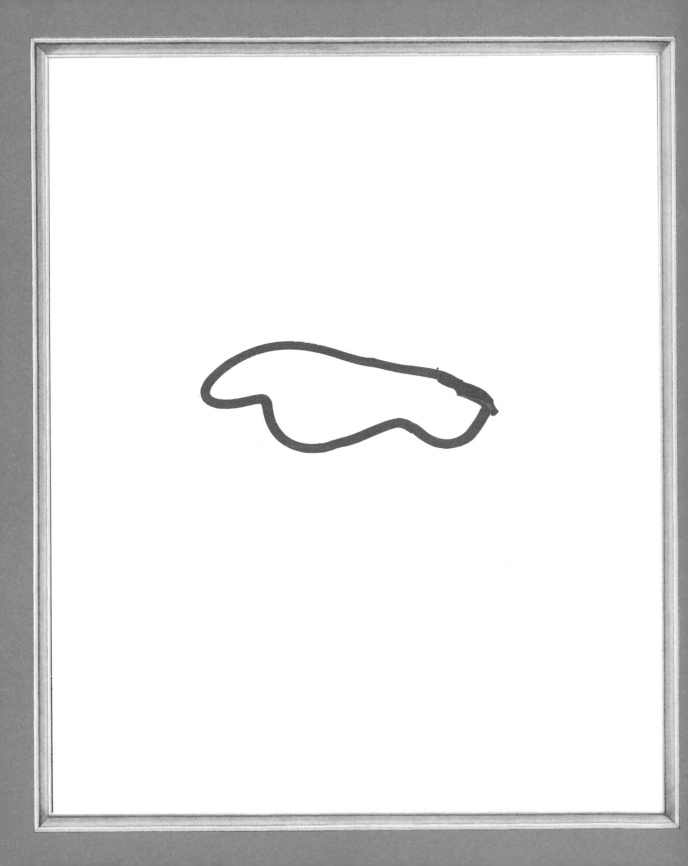

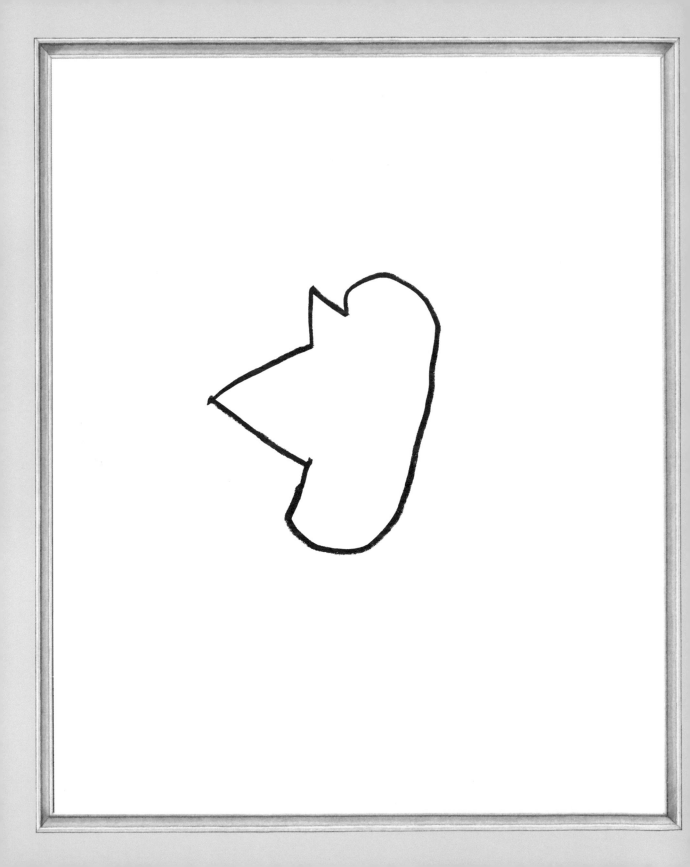

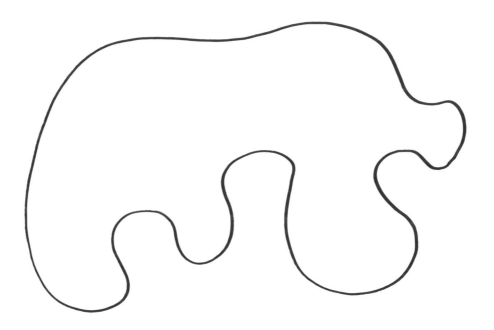

SAM LLOYD

Sam Lloyd

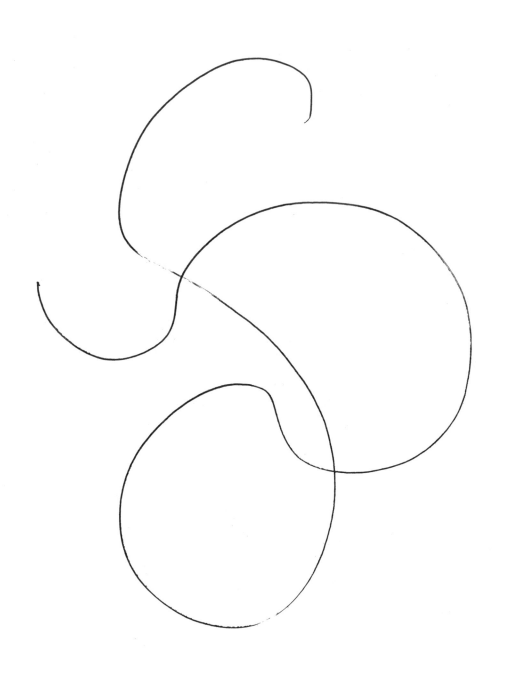

JIM CARTER

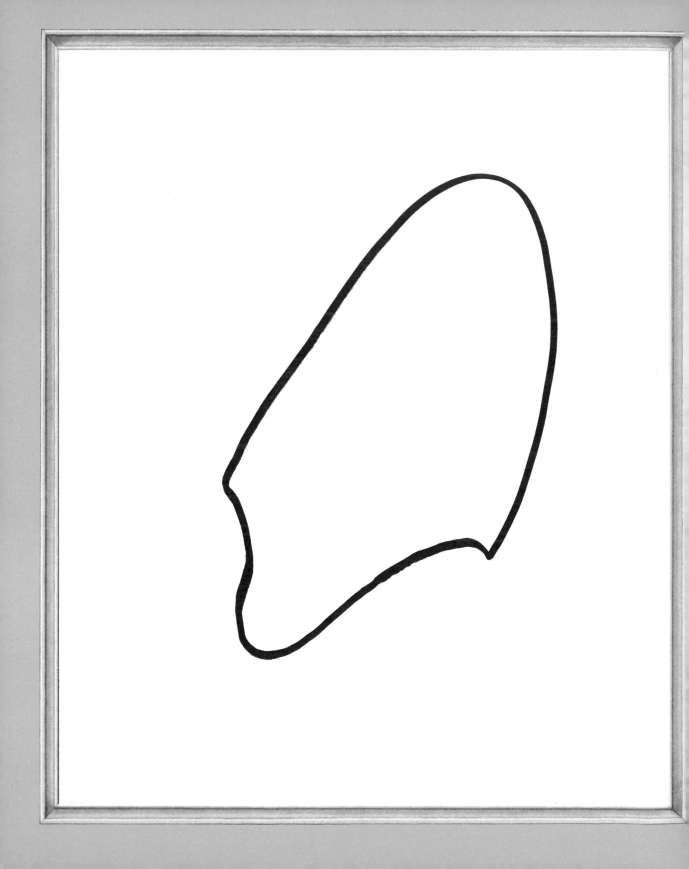

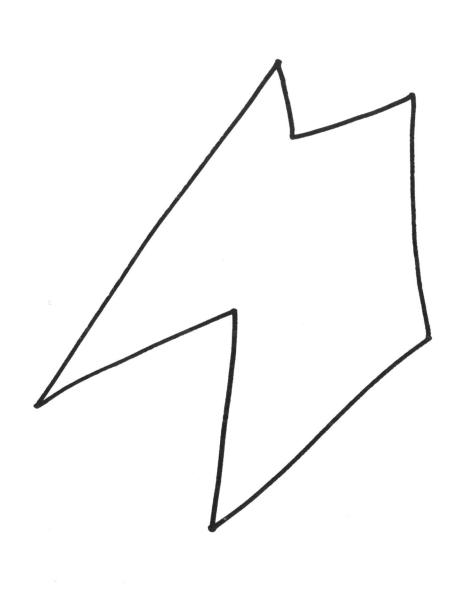

ALEXIS TAYLOR

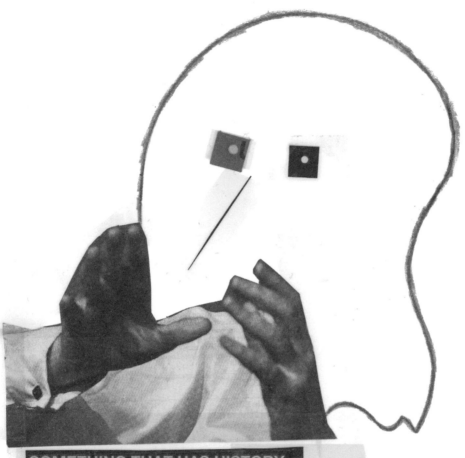

SOMETHING REAL

SOMETHING THAT HAS HISTORY,
THAT HAS A TRADITIONAL SHAPE

FRAGILE MAN

'Moira'   Catherine Rayner

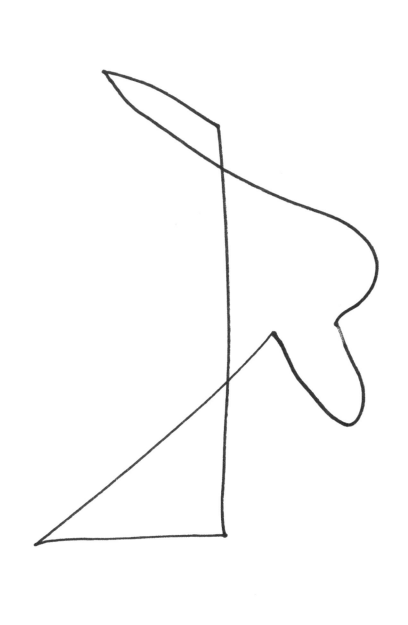

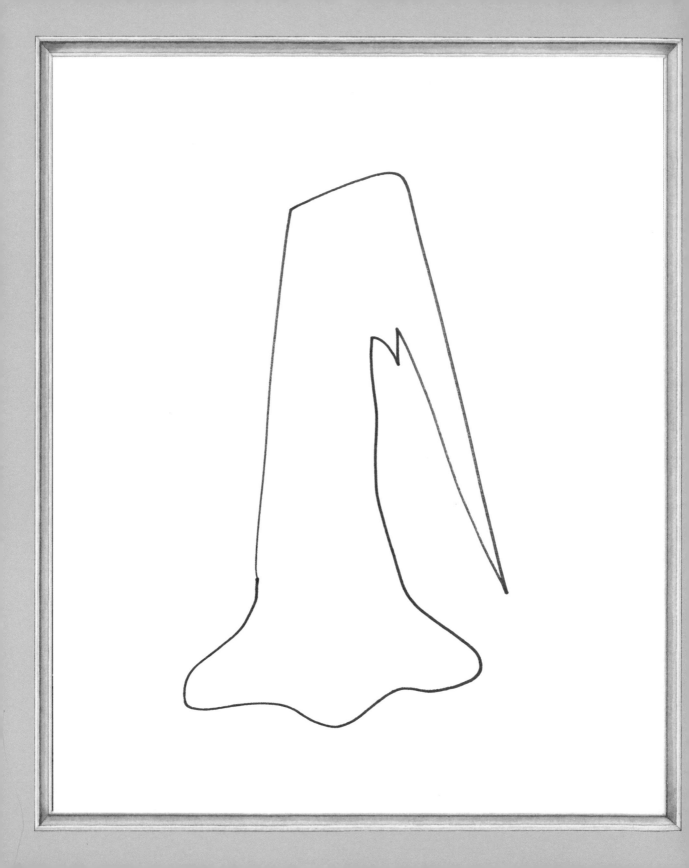

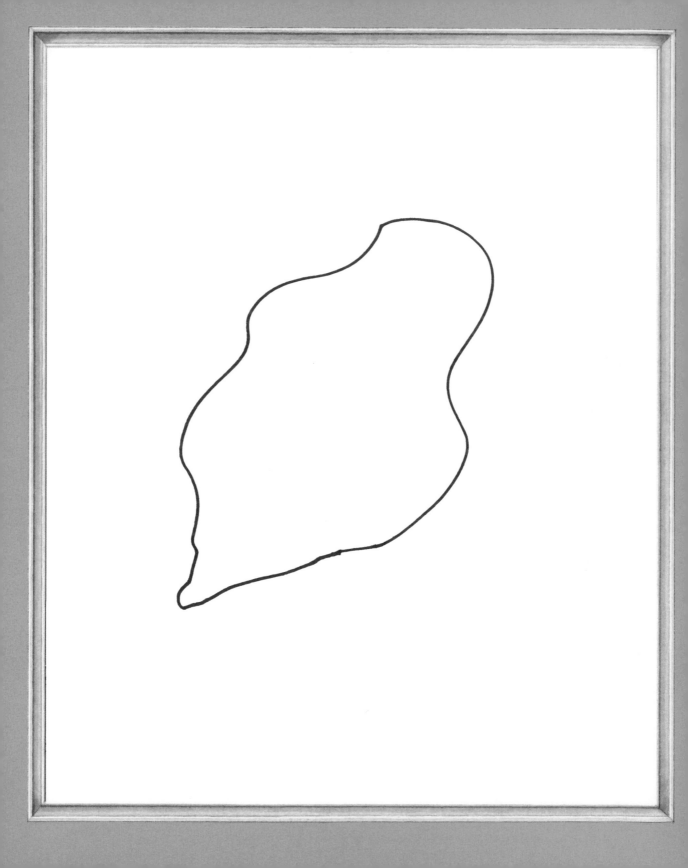

LEIGH FRANCIS

When I grow up I wanna be Teen Wolf

MICHAEL FOREMAN

Hip, Hippo Hooray for the Rainbow Trust!

michaelforeman 2010

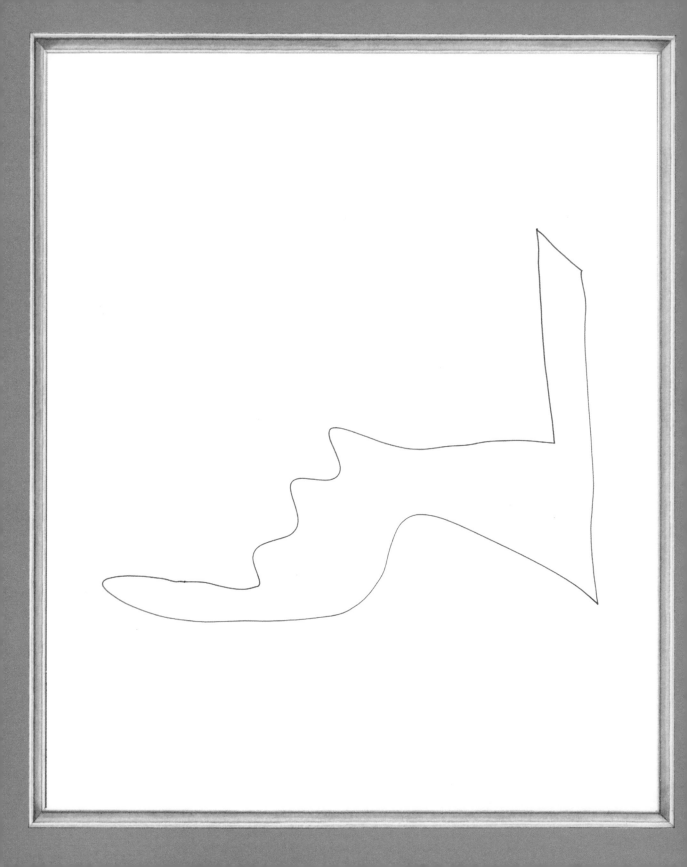

The zombie's house was surprisingly civilised — only a vague bad smell that was mostly covered by the roses planted out back...

Patrick

EMMA THOMPSON

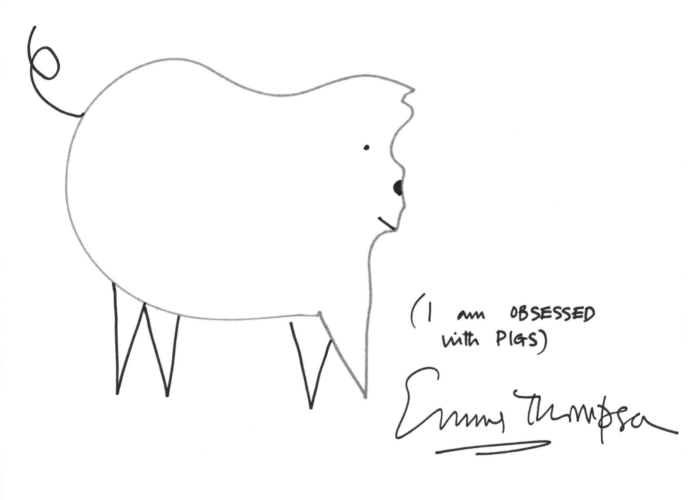

(I am OBSESSED
with PIGS)

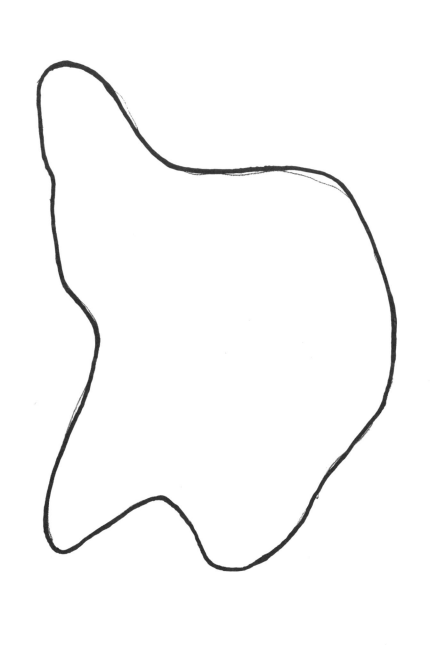

MEERA SYAL

Dandy-Lion

SIR ANDREW MOTION

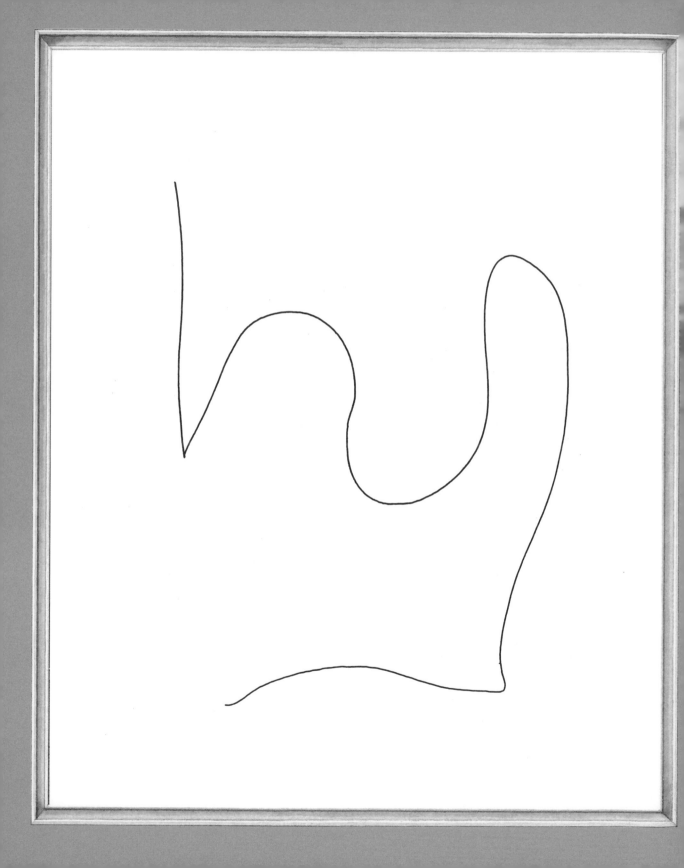

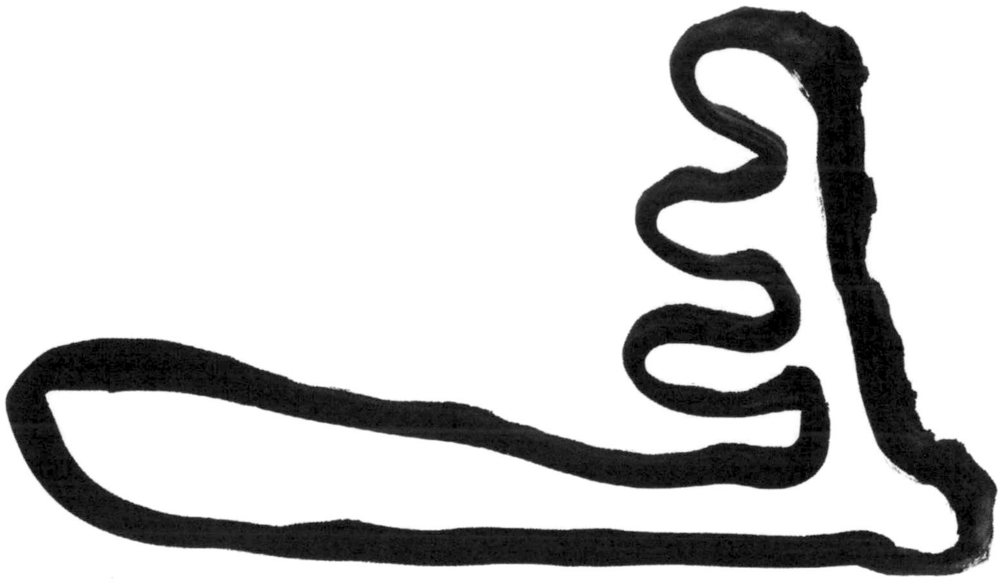

TARA PALMER-TOMKINSON

NICK SHARRATT

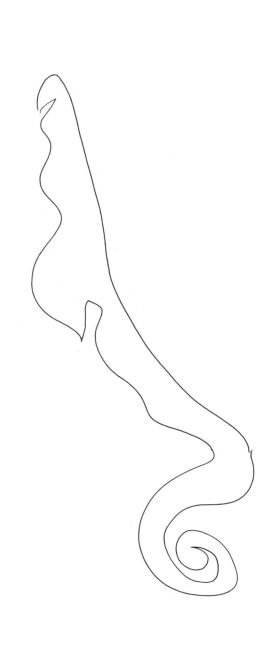

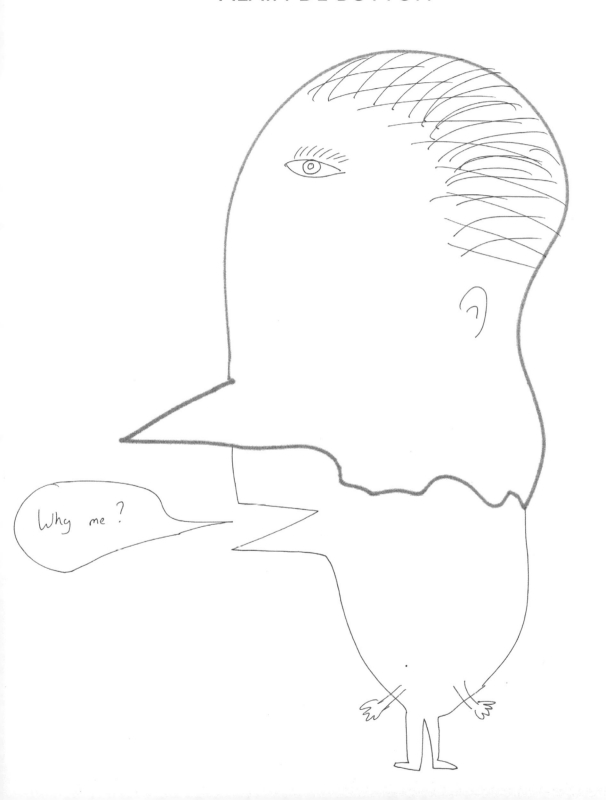

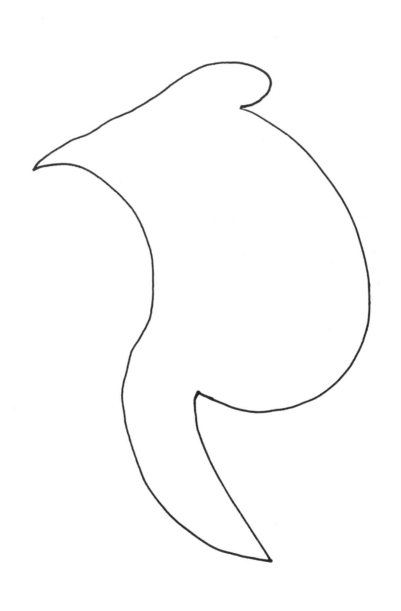

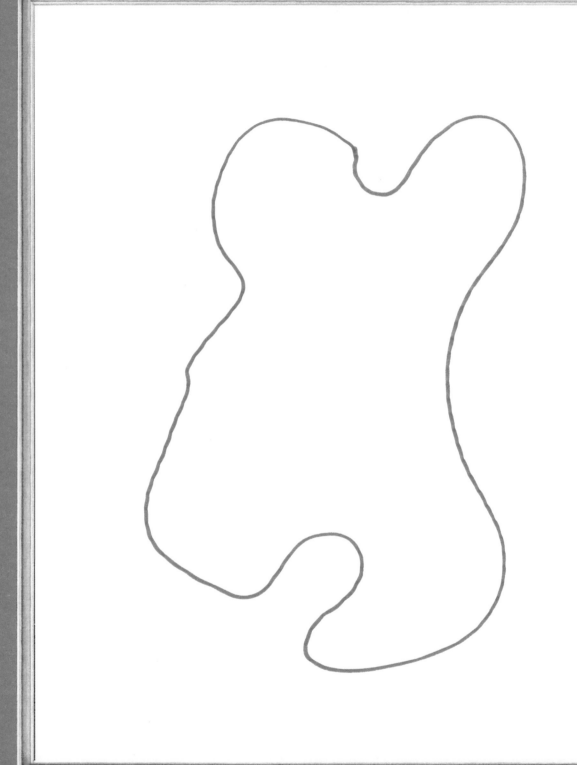

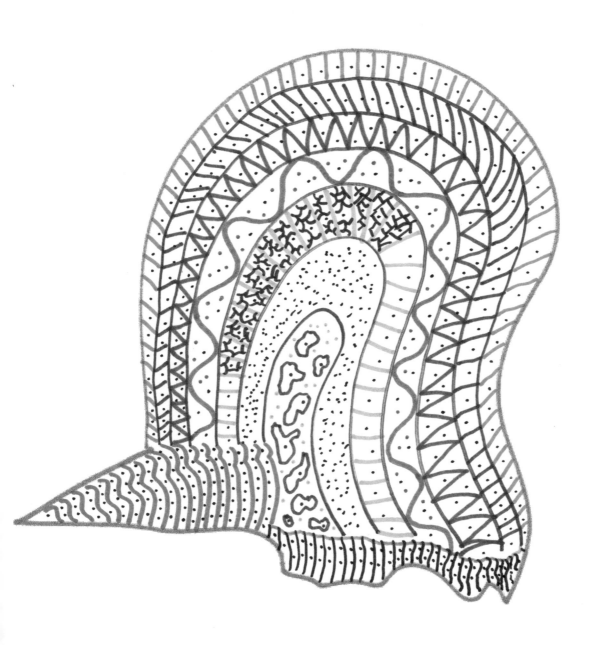

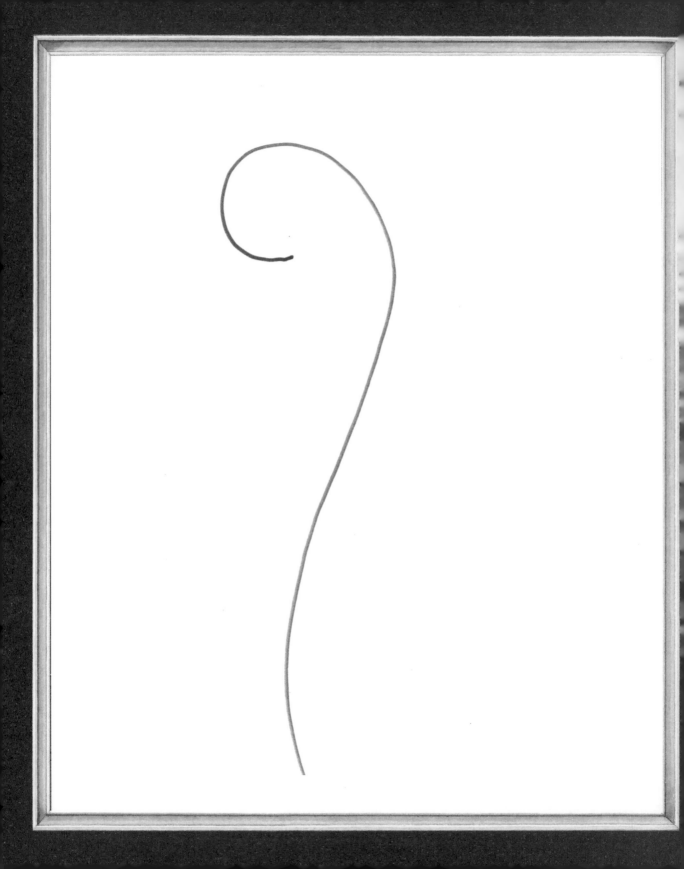

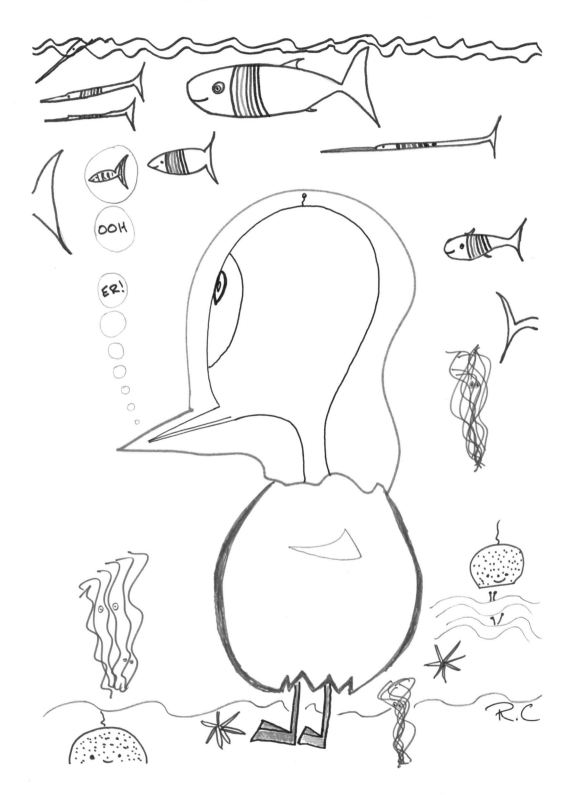

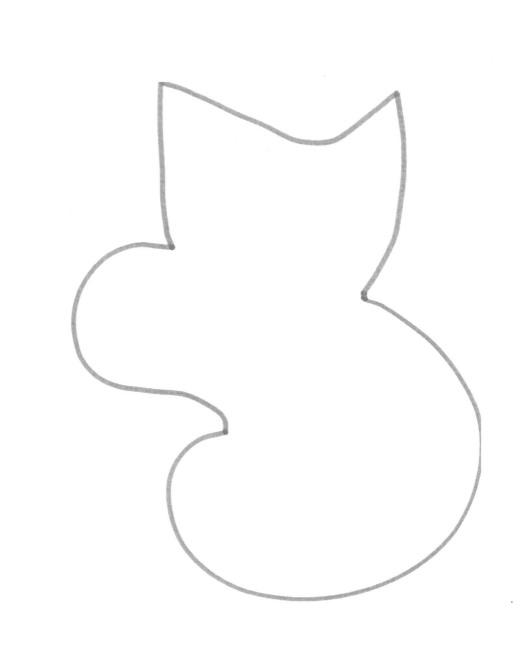

HENRY WINKLER
(The Fonz – who drew his own shape)

It is easier to love a
Rainbow than to catch one
Enjoy your life
Henry Winkler
5/3/10 3³⁰pm
LA.